BEGINNINGS
OVER AND OVER

First published in 2025 by
The Dedalus Press
13 Moyclare Road
Baldoyle
Dublin D13 K1C2
Ireland

www.dedaluspress.com

ISBN 978-1-915629-43-2 (paperback)

Dedalus Press titles are available in Ireland
from Argosy Books (www.argosybooks.ie) and in the UK
from Inpress Books (www.inpressbooks.co.uk).

Cover design and layout: Pat Boran

Dedalus Press receives financial assistance from
The Arts Council / An Chomhairle Ealaíon.

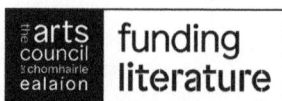

the arts council
§ chomhairle
ealaíon

funding
literature

BEGINNINGS
OVER AND OVER
Four New Poets from Ireland

Mai Ishikawa
Róisín Leggett Bohan
Emer Lyons
Cal O'Reilly

Selected by
LEEANNE QUINN

DEDALUS PRESS

ACKNOWLEDGEMENTS

Acknowledgements and thanks are due to the editors and publishers of the following where a number of these poems originally appeared:

Mai Ishikawa: 'Fibonacci Spiral' was previously published in *Channel.* 'Partition' was first published in *Banshee.* 'Monster' and a version of 'Forest' were previously published in *The Stony Thursday Book.*

Róisín Leggett Bohan: 'Anticipation of Anaphylaxis' and 'Letter to a Lifeguard' were previously published in *The Plaza Prize Anthology.* 'The Somnambulist of Sceilig Mhór' was first published in *Poetry Ireland Review.* 'And I had bought new underwear from Penneys' was first published in *Abridged.* 'The Cryptographer' was previously published in *The Guthrie Gazette.* 'the hearse that stalls on hills' was first published in The Patrick Kavanagh Award anthology, *The Monster's Back.* 'His Coat' was previously published in *The Irish Independent.* 'Exit Music for a Boy' was first published in *Magma Poetry.* 'Birthday' was first published in *Hammond House Anthology.*

Emer Lyons: 'Theoretical Archaeology' and 'I Photocopy Vaginas' were previously published in *The Stinging Fly* in their featured poet segment. 'Elegy for God's Own Country' was first published on *The Spinoff.* 'Tanks' was first published in *The Tangerine.* 'Winter Wood' was previously published on *The Spinoff* and in *The Friday Poem:100 New Zealand Poems.*

Cal O'Reilly: 'The Party' was first published in *Foyle Young Poets of the Year Anthology 2022.* 'Naming' was first published in *fourteen poems.* 'Portbou' was previously published in *Ink Sweat & Tears* and in *Poetry with Pride Magazine* (Belfast Pride). 'India Street' was previously published in *catflap.*

Contents

≈

Mai Ishikawa

Fibonacci Spiral / 13
Pendulum / 14
Partition / 15
The Migration of Theta Waves / 16
Befallen / 17
Kintsugi / 18
Monster / 19
Faceless / 20
Arrow / 21
Forest / 22
Bump-a-dump / 23
The Looking Glass / 24
Sleep that Knits / 25
Unfinished / 26
Our Dreams / 27

≈

Róisín Leggett Bohan

Anticipation of Anaphylaxis / 31
04 C 14598 / 32
The Somnambulist of Sceilig Mhór / 33
The Cryptographer / 34
No and Yes and It's Just You / 36
Letter to a Lifeguard / 38
the hearse that stalls on hills / 40
We Next of Kin / 41

His Coat / 43
Exit Music for a Boy / 44
Birthday / 45
the viewfinder in Chernobyl (2003) / 46

≈)

Emer Lyons

Osclaím na Fuinneoga / 51
Paraphrasing Visions / 52
Theoretical Archaeology / 53
I Photocopy Vaginas / 54
Limbs of Time / 55
Soup / 56
Elegy for God's Own Country / 59
Fortress / 60
A Man-made Sun / 61
Somebody Killed the Cat / 62
Tanks / 63
Mouse/Mice / 64
Winter Wood / 65

≈)

Cal O'Reilly

The Party / 69
Naming / 70
Portbou / 71
India Street / 72
he meets the criteria and will be referred
to the endocrinologist / 73
Portrait / 75
Top Gun / 76

Family Gathering / 77

I went to the library and I didn't think about / 78

Ferry / 79

Comedown / 80

Outing / 81

Lockdown Cycle / 82

Visit / 83

∽

ABOUT THE EDITOR

Leeanne Quinn / 84

INTRODUCTION

'AND BEGINNINGS OVER AND OVER' writes Róisín Leggett Bohan in 'No and Yes and It's Just You'. All writers begin, and then begin again and again. To write is to commit to a lifetime of beginnings on the page. In the process the poem is made new, and poetry – as it continues its trajectory through our current century – is shifted and nudged, a little this way or that. For poetry – and by extension, language – must always change and keep changing. Poetry cannot stay the same. It must be altered, continually. If we are to really begin again, it must even be undermined. The aim of this anthology is to introduce the work of four exciting poets who have taken part in the Dedalus Press Mentoring scheme, and whose bold, formally striking and stylistically innovative writing is part of that change and continuation. Mai Ishikawa, Róisín Leggett Bohan, Emer Lyons, and Cal O'Reilly are writers who are willing to risk, willing to discover, willing to alter and undermine. I have sat with these poems for many months and each has left their mark. I hope the readers of this anthology will feel this same energy and will follow these four gifted poets as they set out – as they commit themselves to begin, over and over again.

—Leeanne Quinn
January 2025

Mai Ishikawa

Mai Ishikawa is a Japanese theatre maker, translator, poet and performer based in Dublin. She has translated several plays into Japanese for full productions. She won the Unohana Prize in the 8th Kyoto Writing Competition and was shortlisted in the Westival International Poetry Competition 2024. Her poems have appeared in *The Stony Thursday Book, Banshee, Channel, Ragaire, The Storms* and *Ink Sweat & Tears*. She incorporates poetry in her theatre work, combining poetic dialogue with physical movement, to suspend time and find the extraordinary in the ordinary.

Fibonacci Spiral

You are held by your mother who
pats your back, like a divine instrument.
You stare down at me, as if

I am a grotesque underground creature.
And I look at you as if I know you.
Then she turns you around

and shows me who you are. Your dome
with coiled grass; sunflower seeds
cuddling one another;

a tornado stirring up sand;
the deep secret of pine cones;
a thousand generations of bees.

You remind me of who I am.
You make me want to crack
the ground over my head.

Pendulum

You say your eyes are tired,
and leave everything to my left hand.

The sea on our left invites us to open.
The forest on our right beckons like a secret.

We are old enough to know both are better seen
from afar, but the child in us sways until the tug-of-war
between our hands is caressed away by the waves or

I must have tightened my grip.
We walk a mile, straight. But then you

gasp like a baby squeezed
out from the safe, tight tunnel,
eyes wide open.

Partition

I sit by a window, with my friend.
 Outside, a girl enters my reflection.

A coffee at my right hand, neglected.
 Her fresh uniform flutters as she giggles.

Cups clanging, taps running, waiters yelling.
 Her gaze slowly opens towards me.

The noise comes to rest.
 We fall into a smile.

A grief descends — a disbelief.
 She turns away, like a closing book.

My friend's voice dials louder.
 The girl recedes further.

The clanging, the taps, the yelling.
 She is out of sight.

I see my own reflection again.
 She has left years on me.

The Migration of Theta Waves

You footfall down the stairs, a morning chime; prelude to chaos.
Fairies laugh and mess your hair as you dream at the kitchen table.

You hold back the tears now, that once ran down like fierce weirs.
Fairies waiting for the mighty rain complain of skin left dry.

You set off for the bitter world, clearing space for science
and love. Fairies shake their heads, pack their things and leave.

Newspaper dangles from my father's hand. Fairies leer and hiss.
A New World! They roll and roll like dogs on his thin, soft hair.

Befallen

As if everything fell to the ground
and anticipation of the sun faded.

As if words withered in your mouth
to empty meanings and dangling sounds.

As if nobody knew your name
and names you knew receded.

As if the *shitake* scent that crossed an ocean
stayed in the cardboard box.

As if you were drawn to the world of birds
and not the words of humans.

As if your face turned yellow
when you faced the streets.

As if you stared at a deafening wind
and walked like a stranger.

As if a robin never explained
where it had been.

As if the autumn wind had risen.

Kintsugi

It's like losing your footing lying in bed,
Or flowers swaying in a windless field.
She can scream in a stranger voice,
As she rocks a baby in her arms.
And you pray that somehow
It will pass, by hanging a weather doll
At the windowsill,
While the dunnock mother feeds
A cuckoo baby bigger than herself
Like a promotion she earned.
As if nobody questions
Why they live on a plate with cracks,
But everyone believes that these
Can be stitched with golden threads.

Monster

January 17, 5:46 am
From under my bed, a huge fist punches me in the back. My mother crawls into my room like a worm. A bookshelf falls flat on its face.

January 18
On the ground floor, we nestle in our futons. Thunderous footsteps overhead. Plates rattle; voices quiver on the phone; on the screen, a neighbourhood burns again and again; Coca-Cola and hamburger ads disappear; and brown water spills from the taps.

January 25
We line up in the school courtyard. Teachers are counting the students. We look at each other in wonder; the world has restarted. My sister's friend is missing. Her shelf also had a heart attack — in the wrong place. Wrong words escape my mouth. Guilt crawls up my throat.

February 25
Near to the epicentre, I walk with my mother. We have brought egg sandwiches. Stores and shops are all shut. The footprints are everywhere. I am numb and deaf and blind, but I can taste my egg sandwich. Vividly.

Faceless

Do you like it here?
Yes, in fact, I do.

Where are you from?
I don't know.

I remember you.
You do? I remember you too.

Maybe we have met.
Maybe we have.

We were on a boat.
That's right.

A boat that ran like a train.
Yes, a boat that ran like a train.

Arrow

You flutter from nowhere and I see a flash;
a delicate compass in your eyes. A trust so deep,
you left the land you held close. Once it flashed

in my own sleep — shooting out to sea —
distinct and faint, against the Tokyo Jungle.
Not my face or my voice — but it was

mine. Straight, and not a tremble of doubt
in its trail. The back view was like an old man's
hunch — not determination but resignation.

I look out the kitchen window as you stretch
your wings. I turn a purple turnip in my hands;
East China Sea, India, Middle East, France —
Ireland.

Forest

Last night I had a dream.
I was asked, *Which vegetable is most likely to sit on a chair?*
I answered, *Tomato* — I was right.
I got a standing ovation.

Last night I had a dream.
I was told, *You are barren.*
I bombed the kitchen sink with forks and knives —
like a hormonal uprising.

Last night I had a dream.
I was asked, *Why did you do it?* over and over.
I said, *Because M told me to,* again and again
till I was told, *M doesn't exist.*

Last night I had a dream.
I gave my friend presents —
thousands and thousands of them.
She began to thin them out, like seedlings.

Bump-a-dump

There is a mushroom in my womb.
It sucks and sucks till I'm doomed.
Consume and make room.

The mushroom grows and plays
Humpty-Dumpty-Boo.
Consume and make room.

Will I consume my womb,
the mushroom in my room?
Would I fly or would I cry?
Consume and make room.

O look how big it has become!
Bump-a-dump, bump-di-boom,
embrace the moonly rite.
Consume and make room.

The Looking Glass

I am travelling down a hole.
I follow and follow
into the Pink Wonderland.

The salt water gently pushing
doors, welcomed by white
anemones, waving.

The walls cupping the cave
are swollen, as if
by discontent that has sunk

deep down, and solidified;
my desires secretly
moulding the wall decor.

I am amazed how some things
just will not disappear —
they harden to survive.

The salt water recedes.
I let go of my breath.
I pray this pain will never

turn to bitterness as I follow
the White Rabbit dangling
his madly ticking watch,

out the exit.

Sleep that Knits

I am most calm in this moment when I pull the curtain
over the world, against the imprints I have left;
all the mess.

I count the things I have done — not sheep — one by one
praising every child in the room as I leave

for home. I am glad that I have done them
finished or unfinished
that I have done them anyway

that I am at last leaving. I shall recline
on the night that sinks into a walk
on a bridge arching over a river to another day

that may or may not be linked to this one, passed on
to myself in another world; me in some other

shape or style.

Unfinished

My mother pots up my poems
in the May sun — one by one.
I say they are finished they are done.
She says they will grow they will flower
as she pats manure
around the roots.

Earthworms swarm over my poem
and infiltrate it — one by one.
They wriggle through words
too glossy for disbelieving hearts.
Fish-eyed, I watch and sigh satisfied
as it breaks apart.
I swim to the crumbling poem
and snatch each word.

I had a poem; a kingdom
where swirling houses
the small and the big and the medium
settled in the right place — one by one.
A path where right and left were
distant twins; a transcription
of my muted mouth.
As my mind seeped
into the pillow, I knew
I was finished.

Our Dreams

Ten years ago, I was the fringe of skirt
dancing in the wind,
refusing to touch the ground.

Now I am in stillness.

Everything has receded like a tide,
baring broken buggies, old tyres,
skeleton bikes. I suspect
that the water was just a dream — which I miss

the way I miss oily chips
the perfume that had me wrong
the heels that bloodied my toes.

These are etched on my senses.
Like nostalgia. Like lies.

Birds walk on the sand and peck for prey;
their lives depend on
our dreams receding.

Róisín Leggett Bohan

∽

Róisín Leggett Bohan is a writer from Cork. In 2024, she was runner-up in the Patrick Kavanagh Poetry Award and Listowel Best Poem Award and was a finalist in the Aesthetica Creative Writing Award. Her work appears in *Poetry Ireland Review, Banshee, Magma, Aesthetica, The Pomegranate London*, and more. Róisín was selected for the Poetry Ireland Introductions series, 2022 and the Seamus Heaney Summer School, 2024. She is a UCC graduate, and *HOWL New Irish Writing* co-editor. Róisín is grateful for a literature bursary from The Arts Council of Ireland and an artist bursary from Cork City Arts.

Anticipation of Anaphylaxis

When you have gone, I will dismantle the air purifier,
rake the remains of your skin cells, sieve you into a pot,
simmer and strain again until you are the consistency
of bone ash, like the cow cortical they use for fine china cups.
I will drink you in so I can appropriate your gravel-voice.
Add the juice of raspberries, anthracite: dress my lids
with your shadow so I can see people in dole queues
with empathetic eyes. Scatter you across gaffer tape, stick
you to my chest and other openings. Remember your wet face
that time you buried our first dog in the rain. Sniff you
in a line, rolling up your last bus ticket, the 208. Smell
the Beamish from your shoes, that first night we met. I'm sorry
I got sick. When I hear *so sorry for your loss* I won't answer
with, *it's the little things I miss.* How you used to slap my ass
when I bent down to unload the dishwasher, or your propensity
for finding abandoned animals: that albino ferret who skittered
up your trouser leg, took too much interest in your crotch.
No. I will say, he is not gone, *I am wearing him.*

04 C 14598

In the fast lane, I catch it in the rear-view mirror. Once my father's car. I indicate, pull into the slow lane — it overtakes me, lights flashing back. The dent in the bumper there still, where my mother backed up a little too much. She was a feather that day, shedding one-week-old grief with weeping, while that woman threw rage in a shopping centre carpark. He was post-surgery, morphined up, my sister and I on night shifts swabbing his nightmares. I'm watching the car boot, wheelchairless. They didn't know what to do when we asked about his leg. My brothers left the hazard lights on while the mortician handed them a long cardboard box. They fastened it in the back seat, drove it to the plot on the mountain, where our farmer neighbours waited, shovels in their welted hands — eased it into earth — 10 years before he'd follow it. At the exit for the hospice, the car races full throttle. I shadow it, far beyond home. Fuchsia roads, dodgy hairpins, catching up but losing ground. I ease my foot off the accelerator. No longer within my view. Figment, ever phantom. Never mine to steer.

The Somnambulist of Sceilig Mhór

We kept our eyes closed so we could see better, in the dark.
Skimming the irises of furze, my linted gloves, and you
buttoned up in my duffle coat sucking on its ivory toggles.

On and up the path to the watching place, the thrifts and campion
waved sleep at my ankles. I carried you. Up the six hundred steps
etched into granite, ribbing the parabolic curve of cliff.

Above the warbling weight of gannets that marbled our ears.
You barked back at the monks in their beehive huts, humming
scriptures amongst the gurgle and dive of kittiwakes,

basking sharks. And the unknowing yawn of this moment made you
nip at my fingers with your soon-to-be-gone teeth. As the monks
sang in slow drifts, we opened our lantern eyes with matchsticks.

*Note: In days gone, lighthouse keepers would often keep their eyes shut
and their lamps unlit upon waking so as to maintain their night
vision for the night watch.*

The Cryptographer

for Ariel, resident cat of Tyrone Guthrie Centre,
Annaghmakerrig

We carried the summer
in our mouths. Nightwalks.
You padding behind, belly
dipping the tips of dandelion seeds.
Ardent expeditionist, your slinky trot
followed by a sudden
sprint-gallop, out of nowhere
your electric whiskers
bunting every sprouting
thing: ankles of trees, sleeping buttercups.
That fawn moth you played
with, let go — watched it beat upward
before you rolled on your back, as if to say:
I give you this, only this — take it
your mitts aloft, swatting clouds.
You taught me to pause, listen
to bustling shafts of long
grass; the bending backs
of rushes, sift of branches
murmuring above us
reminded me that chaos
becomes too tricksy
at times, you offered me your magnetic eyes:
nocturnal vision, until I got my bearings
with beauty I was not made to see.
You took my ink-hand
blotted with limp words
down to the boathouse, where water
lisped and eddied through pockets

of the boat slip. And as evening
slapped up rain you rowed the currach
out to the middle of the lake.
We inhaled the quiet landing
before you mewed in Morse code
imagine if we could forgive ourselves everything.

No and Yes and It's Just You

after Meghan O'Rourke

No, no veils, more a flare from a vessel
that singed my eyes. And cliff-grass, yes, knee-deep —
dandelion seed-sift, buttercups like little lifejackets.

My mother, yes, I thought of her hands —
all they had done — for four small seconds.

No virus, more like a cough closing
in over my lungs, negating breath.
      No software, no flicker, more a pinging flash –
      lightbulb giving way.

And beginnings over and over.
Yes. It was like that.

No gas station food but I tasted everything I touched.
      And yes, it was a long and mind-bending trip!

And yes, there is sun here — milky and forgiving.
      No punishment, just my own — always been my thing.
      No drones, but swallows fall asleep in this sky.
      And yes, growth.

No blackouts, the odd bit of fog with morning.

      And yes. I still created you. Your first day? You cried
      for three hours non-stop — but you fell quiet
      when I carried you to the trees — the stream.

No, we were one at the start
and two at the ending.

   And yes, an entrance —
   we were always that.

Yes, we stood in that room
with no words — the hum of heat
between us. And yes, we looked
at the painting but saw different things.

Yes, the snow nibbled
at our toes, but we imagined
Saharan hot sand — remember?

And yes, our names were not the same
but always ours. And yes. I love(d) you —
you did not misunderstand.

   No, it's not terrible, there are books.

And I'm sorry —
I don't intend to return.

No, it's only you
I hear keening.

And yes. I will stay all the nights.

Letter to a Lifeguard

And I was wondering if you'd like to go scuba diving. You have to go down in pairs. Something to do with the oxygen. I suppose if that rubber tube in your mouth detached then maybe I'd need to — resuscitate you? Although to tell you the truth, I wouldn't be an expert in mouth-to-mouth, especially underwater. But there's all that bright fish and plankton and if we reached the seabed, we might spot a lobster, did you know they can live for 100 years? Imagine what they've seen? Oil spills, shipwrecks, fishing nets heavy with friends, and the wars, did I mention my dad was in a war? Once he saw a boy's head break open from shrapnel and twice, he heard the captain shout *full steam ahead boys* while the waves washed over burning men. And just because my dad was in the war doesn't mean I'm ancient. I'm the second youngest of seven children and my dad married late and my mother was much younger and did I mention that I nearly drowned once when I was five and no one saw because my mother was front-heavy with my sister and I suppose I felt like the wet tomato sandwiches with the sand in them, the way they'd disintegrate in your hands shivering with sunburn in that navy bathing suit; the little silver anchor hanging heavy from the waist belt weighing me down. And did I say that I don't like wearing bathing suits and that in fact I don't like swimming in public at all? That day at Tralispeen, my older cousin pointing at my chest and laughing with his bad teeth to the other older cousins about my jutty-out pieces and I ran behind the car and covered myself with that faded blue towel and never properly learned to swim because I didn't know there were parts of yourself you had to keep hidden from other people or they might mock you and like it at the same time if you were a girl wearing boys' shorts when you thought it was all alright. No one said no one said no one said no one said you were supposed to be something else.

And I had bought new underwear from Penneys

with my pocket money, blue and yellow-flowered trimmings.
Primroses? Or was it ever spring then? No. It was cold under the
hiss of gaslight, spitting orange flares, shivering still in that one-
bedroomed flat. I had just read you my story for school in which
you featured as the main character — suited man undertakes
apprentice. I sat on the edge of the bed wishing less freckles for
my knees as you burned my initials into your arm with a
cigarette and the smell of my name on your person made me
sick after I had said *this doesn't feel right.*

the hearse that stalls on hills

night spins, ever.
you in the back, buckled up
in oak, tucked in crimson velvet.
a vintage motor, dodgy
to handle: steering
gets stuck, indicators point us
in the wrong direction.
cracks in the roof where the rain
gets in. we are in floods, often.
I fasten life vest to your thin chest
wishing windscreen wipers for my eyes.
solemn hitchhikers offer to share the wheel
but only I know this journey:
haphazard bends, black spots, the donuts you beg me to
do over! do over! do over!
days are tarpaulin — but
night spins, ever.

We Next of Kin

meet in elevators
of the hospital.
As swift as sparrow
sex we slip in and out, hatch
plans: how best to navigate nurses —
less snippy, more *we are not worthy*.
We stalk consultants and their fledglings.
Do the rounds of hugs
swabbing our night-shift
eyes on the shoulders of others.
We lament over bulging catheters,
extra-vasating cannulas. Practise
kneeling at the altar of the kitchen
staff for jelly pots and non-plastic
spoons. Whisper the sadness
of DNR stickers while the tinnitus
of alarming monitors
becomes our looped-track.
We recognize recruits from the scented-steam
of their orange bags — yoghurt
and urine-muralled pyjamas.
We sneak Beamish and Poitín
into sippy cups to curb and counter
pain. We go off-campus, seek
alternative lifts: shopping centre
car parks, council offices, high-rise flats.
Yellow-beamed buttons flash
before us: 23, 66, 94 —
on we go, higher and faster
until our chests surge
upward, arms outward,
we are swarm of starlings:

circling air currents,
kiting thermals, holding hands —
waiting for our loved ones to arrive.

His Coat

I do not wear it now,
within the ox-blood lining
there was an inside pocket
and in it I hid his voice.
I used to slip my fingers
in and take it out,
watch the soft palate undulating,
enunciating misshapen words.
I would hold it up to my ear,
hear its bending rhythm, its pace
as unsteady as a small vessel in a swell.
I placed it under my nose once, inhaled its sound,
its smell lay somewhere between honeysuckle and pipe tobacco.
I wanted more — his tone, his fluency, his articulation,
to feel the rush of air through his vocal cords.
I pushed it into my mouth.
It balanced on my tongue before I tried to swallow
but my mouth gaped open like an unfilled grave
spluttering the words 'let' and 'go'.
I caught them — before they fell, stitched them
up within the folds of my lips.
Swollen, an inky exudate seeped
through the cracks of my infected vermillion.
I have ruined my pout. I don't eat, just sip
iced rum through a straw to anaesthetise —
the pain isn't all that bad
if I don't speak.

Exit Music for a Boy

i.m. N. L.

Always you to shape a quiet exit
out back doors of parties
I'd watch you leave over
some slow-dancing shoulder.
Always you, me — *best friends*
coming off shift, splitting a greasy
breakfast, your drowsy mouth
grinning as you played with the biro
stuck in my night-duty hair.
Always you to be sidetracked: falling
from my window, your eyes averted
to tanned limbs of girls on the cricket pitch.
You broke your leg; I pushed you to the pub
and back for weeks — our tipsy-laughs tripping
potholes, the hospital stacks throwing us bad shapes.
Always you to conceal your leaving, slipping hushed — gone.
The silence slapped me like a siren, sometimes I hear you
laugh as I pass the recovery room.

Birthday

nails erode open, earth
seeps itself inside me,
burrow through to find
you, dig until I hit wood
but cannot open your door.
wake up now! I call out.
you emerge in crisp
white and paint your lips
with my blood. I plant
a kiss on your forehead,
face freckled with mud.
hello petal! I cry out.
longing to blanket
you with my love
but I fail once more,
forget to remember —
I cannot nourish you
ever. tracing the seams
of your once possibilities.

the viewfinder in Chernobyl (2003)

no sense of a season here

air — stagnant   swallowed   by the weight
    of a place name

my boots cough up dirt   navigate an uneven path
    one eye

in the viewfinder   the other   scanning
    the next shot

sun-stained handle   of a waterspout   droops beside
    an empty bucket

the   silver   birches   stand   quiet

I log — timecode   close-ups   caesium levels
    my clothes   in yellow hazard bags

you   *will*   *burn*   *after*   *this*

film camera   on my shoulder   captures

Gomel asylum   Novinky orphanage   The Red Zone

record   play   *erase*

the best shots — that child's smile   sunset in the
    minibus   mirror

sifted light   through the bars   of a window

refraction   in a glass   of water

water you are advised not to drink

Emer Lyons

⁓

Emer Lyons was a Play it Forward Fellow with Skein Press in 2024 working on an experimental memoir, small town quare, with her mentor Pascal O'Loughlin. She has performed poetry as part of the 2025 Scene + Heard festival in Dublin. Her work has appeared in *Poetry Ireland Review, The Stinging Fly, Banshee* and *The Stony Thursday Book.* She was awarded an Agility Grant by the Arts Council Ireland in 2024.

Osclaím na Fuinneoga

Open the Windows

I wait at the other side to start believing you've moved on
moved back into creation
once I've flown into your sky and married memory
I want to heel parts of my broken
parts lost in the end to prescriptions
I don't think I've spoken more to any other person
yet here I am left with so much to know and tell
I'll go to the graveyard and hope for your/my grand/
great-grand/mother
peel her dirt into my cracks
      is there some of you left behind for me?

Paraphrasing Visions

there was only one chance —
to break, to be broken, to be stronger

i didn't know it then, that the end would come
much as imagined and i would be glad

climb aboard the middle of this night shift
tradition around here is a mass of memorabilia

of the unknown, of the remarkable —
wild wonders have bizarre tail feathers

mourners come
chanting about sacrifice

[i heard some-
times your voice

but you were
not there

just the debris
of a flashback]

Theoretical Archaeology

standing on the fire escape outside our apartment
i look through the window at you

i've spent all day thinking about getting knocked down
and about that one group archaeological trip i went on in
university

when we went underground, or we talked about going
underground …
into a tunnel carrying our pencils so we could crack them in
half to ward off badgers

i was smoking at the time

after that i went on trips alone, walking for miles into the
countryside outside my town trying not to get knocked down
on blind corners

o, i did survey a castle with someone once
inside people smoked joints while we carried around
clipboards and measuring tape

i shout all this through the window at you over the traffic noise
just because i'm telling you the truth, doesn't make it real

I Photocopy Vaginas

frame them
salon-style
pin ceramics to paper
watch the brand-new moon
strongest of the year
makes me think
you are hiding things in buckets
i belong in the hallway
with the parsley
making everything stick
i'm going to put a christmas tree
on the fire escape
blame it for my death
i think of all the people
i don't want to talk to
in the new year
i feel clean
forget that i never learnt
to wash myself
the pictures taken from the floor
piece together like cake
i know you are out there
i say into the darkness
this time i'll see you coming

Limbs of Time

i wanted to take you home
    but i was still living with my ex
        the joy of roles at the beginning
            me pretending to eat breakfast
                and you pretending to stay up past nine thirty
                    then it escalated cross country
                        until i'm standing outside our apartment
                            where we had to take the door off its hinges
                        to accommodate the dream desk
                    for your room of your own
                while i had a desk
            in the corner of the living room
        i'd have taken up arms for you
    sewed them to my sides
        they would have decomposed
            while you flourished
                like the succulents
                    who outlived me
                        and i miss those plants
                    more than you

Soup

your name in my mouth
        a rawness worn out from calling
brain proteins frozen by your eyes
        & i can't accept this mourning
w/all that being in love
        & forgetting how many times i was too much
we shrunk down like woollens
        all the tiny things we took travelling
the heart chakra is green
        i tell this to myself
as the trainee hairdresser goes in a third time w/the bleach
        i wonder about the eroticism of hair
it getting all tangled in mouths
        disturbing intimacy
the kind of intimacy that is not sex
        the kind of sex that is not sexuality
some people think i'm lying when i say i've brown eyes
        but they change in the light
like everything

is that what love is?
wake in the morning
& don't turn away
it's hard to remember now
w/all that built up dirt
i never cleaned from the shower
& the questions about taking a mop
to the roof
& the way i miss the pot plants

in YIN Saskia is telling stories again
the sinews of my muscles find space
        extend beyond me
draw back to become
        dragon
boat
        cat
cow
        flat on my back in between
the air entering the pores i close w/cold water
        you were better at sharing than me
always filling everything up

six days later
& two packs of cigarettes
i'm choking inside
        gulping menthols down like water
but i'm nowhere near the sea
        i'm behind you & we're not speaking
is this how it is after?
        you making soup
& me pretending
        i take it upon myself to become less
so the space i fill up becomes the kind of silence I can bear
        don't talk to me about hope
it brings about a sadness like
        months of longing in drizzling fog
so much talk across all those near-extinct rocks + metals
        i can't remember the name of
here i am w/still only five chords   afraid of repeating the same
    ole thang
maybe we could lick peace off the floor
    it sounds so simple to say that what i miss about you most

is the back of your head
sometimes i wonder why we never fucked in the kitchen
o this wasn't meant to be no sad poem
but that's what you get when you cut everything up

Elegy for *God's Own Country*

i too remember the sea of my insides waving at my face
but why would anyone want to tame a magpie?

it was during the gorse burn
the intimacy of your hands as delicate as with newborn lambs

i'm afraid of the loneliness of poetry without you —
what if inside is more drizzle than rain?

there were days before when danger was a lake of cold water
and to think i was afraid of jumping in

your Dad's not getting any better
people are always telling me things i already know

Fortress

i think about letting it go
this keep of my own making —
but then what else would i be doing?
nothing can mean more than yesterday's missed direction
you repeated something you had already said
that i want to be passed to the next person
like my white linen shirt
with a careful touch
& no hard feelings
to be pleasing
always
always
to be pleasing
& no hard feelings
with a careful touch
like my white linen shirt
that i want to be passed to the next person
you repeated something you had already said
nothing can mean more than yesterday's missed direction
but then what else would i be doing?
this keep of my own making —
i think about letting it go

A Man-made Sun

I saw enough of days.
The mouth rose over the top
in a quiet beauty
behind bloody & bruised dreams —
a fluid coating for destruction.

The guide says I better come back in
May,

If only I could capture it.
By last year it was nearly at the water's edge —
the war believed to be within

in the time of the apple blossoms, the
nightingales.

The walls & floors tore apart.
I let them leak
& they warmed the whole planet.
I tried to wedge a piece
of plywood into the wall to shore it up.
The striking things still
leached from the rock.

I tell her I will.

So far
the impact seems much smaller
than breathtaking.

I believe I will. I
have to believe that.

Somebody Killed the Cat

we shave off our eyebrows in mourning
filter the day to perfection
the bush like ash bagged up from the fire
the smoke-cascading water

we sit in rooms
paintings of people afloat
in boats of their own culture
hang off centre
nobody has legs below the knee

don't leave me here alone
with only the sound of the dog howling
you are the only person who remembers
giving the fish space to flail on the rocky beach
sitting on barrels
babies on our chests
the only person
on the train made of timber
leading the way into the scratching light
far from our eyelashes trembling

i can't look directly at anything
that might hurt to remember
that we were once so close
we wanted our eyeballs to touch

Tanks

Perhaps one day I'll live again around the corner in a room
as empty as this.
—Jean Rhys, *Good Morning, Midnight*

do you have somewhere i could go?
>> where i could hold my own weight + not feel it

jacob's ladder is a set of steps
>> is a recovery programme

if in this place we drink drops of water measured out in beakers
>> i'll think of you in the green light

thank you for braving the outside work for me
>> even if you are on the run from the law

these people they'll cut down trees right on top of you
>> they won't care when your whereabouts are unknown

Mouse/Mice

We refer to the mouse but really it's mice with the traps full every morning this week. My mother says they like chocolate. She takes squares from the bar in the fridge that I bought for myself. It doesn't matter to her because she's off all sweet things for the month of November. For the Holy Souls. For her soul. The mouse, mice, make holes in the corner of my bag of porridge oats. I only notice after eating a bowl. I only notice when oats coat the kitchen drawer. It's too late then not to think about the mouse's insides in my insides. The mouse's taste on my buds. Only then do I throw the bag away. I put a new bag in a different drawer hoping that in the morning I won't find holes. In the bag of oats. In myself. I hear them every morning. Dying somewhere out of sight. I throw their bodies into the wheely bin because I don't know where else to put them. I wake up early to try and intercept the post so my mother doesn't see the deluge of parcels. The mouse, the mice, must know. They are judging me. They are in cahoots with my mother. I imagine their souls rising from the wheely bin. I remember my friend asking where in the body our souls were. We were both brought up to believe souls were worth saving. I wanted to search the inside of my friend's body. I wanted to know that there was a place for me and my friend. And the mouse, the mice. Forever.

Winter Wood

Someone is chopping wood outside my window
or is it loudly inside my head?
the slow swish of the axe
the sharp splinter scattering little shards
impossible to clean up

I want to burrow beneath the soil
lie under the heavy comfort
of the world's body weight
in coffined silence

I have these postcards I frame
images for tourists who know nothing of a place
to send to their families and friends
who know even less

a courier driver asks me to shut his van door
why me? the street is full with the kind of people
who talk to other people
when you call them on the phone

I search my face for trustworthiness
in the hotel room mirror
I have to crouch to look into it

I should feel reassured
when the computer tells me I am not a robot
instead I feel more mechanical than ever
where are all the wayward children?

the chopped wood is stacked
in a neat cascading pile against the side of the house

like a cat bringing home a bird
I can provide it says
blood congealing in its fur

Cal O'Reilly

Cal O'Reilly is a writer from Wexford currently studying at Queen's University Belfast. His recent poems can be found in *fourteen poems, catflap, Ink Sweat & Tears* and *Poetry with Pride* (Belfast Pride). He is an alumnus of the Foyle Young Poets of the Year award, the Edna O'Brien Young Writers Bursary, the T.S. Eliot Prize Young Critics Scheme and the Freedom to Write project by the John Hewitt Society and PEN na hÉireann. He is currently working towards a first pamphlet.

The Party

after Jack Underwood

In the room full of people
I want to be the sort of person you'd turn to
if you entered the room blindfolded.
Or at least the one who wears
shyness like a handwritten invite.
I'd like to have her laugh
which erupts like a broken hose
fixing at the wrong time, or his shoulders
which people love to lay their heads on.
While my skin is sunburnt sea yours is ice-cubes
in grape juice, and I try to think of something
to say but my gut twinges like a dampened
string when you walk over and sometimes
I want to curl my knees to my chest and crawl
inside a guitar so I don't say anything stupid.

Naming

after Remi Graves

I pull on names like shirts/ toss them like coins into the mirror/ the first person I say it to/ is a stranger with soft hair/ and a top-floor apartment/ back home I'm a waterlogged field/ my old name a drenched coat/ scrunched under a bus seat/ at work I count the times I'm called mate instead of love/ every day is just a placeholder/ until it isn't/ I don't know who I'm apologising to/ when I swerve muscle memory/ onto a track/ as softly gravelled as the throat I want/ body as forward slash/ transition or be forever in the next room/ trying to hear yourself think/ I catch my breath running/ the first time you say my name/ a feeling/ fills my chest/ like a room I can stand in/ so bright/ I don't need to look past it

Portbou

Hiking in a binder was a shit idea,
my lungs reach to surface, come short.
There's a sweat mirage on the camera,
a baked red brick rubbed
on the back of my calves
A road you'd find in a motorbike advert
winds down to the sea, too far
below to hear. Cicadas sing
with their whole bodies, all-round
vision hidden in the scrub.
Just when I think I've gone wrong
daubs of paint show the trail
ascending still. I reach
the ridge. The sea is so blue
I want to show it to someone.

India Street

The tattooist's arm is pressed on mine
to keep it steady. Tiny needles
puncture through the purple-inked stencil.
It feels like a meditation. I stare at the edge
of the overhead light — it's already March.
Hallway of my body, waiting
between appointments. But yesterday
walking home in the soft rain
I felt better than I have in months
for no reason I can pin down.
I think this means I've missed you
long enough to know how time moves.
It's my first spring with this name,
next spring I'll have weekly injections,
a room spilling amber light,
but sometimes all I want
is your head on my shoulder.
I consider being honest with everyone.
I want to feel like this all the time
black t-shirt, rolled-up
sleeve, ink settling under
my clingfilmed skin.

he meets the criteria and will be referred
to the endocrinologist.

he doesn't know if he knew at that stage.
he recalls being seven in the lashing rain, hurl-thud
through shin-guards grappling for the sliotar.
that doesn't have to mean anything but it could.
we have mined his childhood for proof.
his mother recalls a daughter.
he was more outgoing as a child.
he was sad when.
he had a happy childhood.
he wishes he grew up in a city.
when he was twelve he stopped eating for two years.
sometimes he cries at teenage boys in films.
the first time he bled, two fingers at the back of his throat.
he described the feeling never washing off.
back pressed to bathroom doors trying to breathe.
he has left home and lived in his chosen gender for a year.
it is important to note that a diagnosis
represents a snap-shot in time.
he was happy wearing dresses as a child.
he feels the need to explain this.
he would like to wear more bracelets.
if he had to pin it down it would be
the 2011 Wimbledon Final, Djokovic v Nadal,
the first person he wanted to look like.
he recalls feeling very strongly
a fly thudding its full body weight into a window pane.
he has demonstrated commitment to his transition.
he is in the process of changing his name by deed poll.
he has considered the irreversible effects.
he has decided against freezing his eggs.

this has been discussed across multiple sessions.
having discussed his entire sexual history.
we have identified a persistent incongruence.
his discomfort meets our criteria.
there are no risks or safeguarding issues.
he described getting into the wrong car,
embarrassed when he had to get out.
he has agreed that his future self would understand.
he wants a future self.
he rated his pain on our multiple scales.
he lay on the hallway floor for long enough to be sure.

Portrait

after Simon Armitage

his hair was an unsanded plank of mahogany
and his eyes were autumn leaves mid-air
and his blink was a duck dipping under
and his teeth were flowers lined at a wall
and his bite was a promontory fort
and his nostrils were a flamenco fan
and his mouth was a sea cavern at low tide
and his smile was a hammock
and his tongue was a forgotten hitchhiker
and his laugh was a roundabout with no exit
and his headaches were lids screwed on too tight
and his arms were damp tomato plant stems
and his wrists were mugs hanging from hooks
and his handshakes were a leg lifted out of the bath
and the palms of his hands were jetliners
and his thumbs were postboxes
and his heart was a seashell
and his lungs were an open-topped car
and his bellybutton was a dandelion clock
and his hips were elbow rests on the train
and his blood system was a mystery novel
and his legs were lampposts at night
and his knees were inverted potholes or macadamia nuts
and his ligaments were Blu Tack left in the press
and his calves were a horse's belly
and the balls of his feet were quicksand
and his secrets were crabs' claws crushed at the beach
and his footprints were the seconds after a movie ends

Top Gun

after Em Power

these bros wear matching aviator shades,
they motorbike to the Air Force base
hands clasped around each other's waists.
these bros play football on the beach in jeans
sweat gleaming in oversaturated bronze lighting.
they have a song that's just theirs — heads bent
together singing 'Great Balls of Fire' at the bar.
they flash a grin and all of San Diego crashes
into the sea. trauma looks hot on them.
they swap bomber jackets and make digs.
they put their lives in each other's hands
white-knuckled. they're fast as in speed
and fast as in stuck fast. these bros
do 200 press-ups to prove a point.
their enemy is an unnamed foreign enemy.
these bros save the world and barely even die.
they're really shouting I LOVE YOU
from the drowned sound of the cockpit.
they climb out of the plane in a grinning daze,
then slam together, chin locked to shoulder,
fists knocking backs. I want this to be queer.
they're still knocking on each other's backs
like a door could swing open and they could
step through, fly literally into the sunset
as 'Hold My Hand' fades into the credits.

Family Gathering

somebody else made
small talk with my
relatives my thoughts
scabbed over I picked
them off one by one I
scraped my stomach
with the small side of
the grater and passed
someone the salt the
walls got tired of
standing and all my
past selves came
tumbling through but
nobody noticed they
were busy shaking
hands my mind is a
tennis court sometimes
everyone goes home
and the floodlights are
left on

I went to the library and I didn't think about

your thigh pressed against mine in the pub
or your head on my shoulder or our hands
intertwined I didn't think about holding you
or about your tongue in my mouth
I didn't think about the texture of your hair
or your stubble on my cheek
or my face pressed into your neck
I didn't think about waking up with my arm
on your chest and your arm heavy on mine
I didn't replay breakfast with you the pastry
crumbs on your shirt I didn't think about
anything you do with your hands
like pouring coffee or playing guitar
I didn't think about you or your laugh
or the way you say *darling* when you're drunk
I didn't think about you when I walked past
the old cemetery wall we talked about climbing over
last October at 2 am I didn't think I saw you
on the bus passing by I didn't think I saw you

Ferry

you can rush to distract yourself or to get somewhere/ now I'm on a Flixbus in the middle of the sea/ I'd rather feel like myself someplace new/ earl grey tea sloshing against a cardboard cup/ thoughts slalom kayaking on a stream pressed to my skin/ once I had the worst conversation and I'm still here/ it's not a choice but I have to choose anyway/ I'm too tired to fully explain right now/ we've arrived/ congratulations a new week/ for now I'll walk and walk/ hang sunglasses from my shirt/ there's a small biscuit with my coffee/ and the waiter is the first person I've spoken to all day/ I could try out a name/ check it in with my hostel key card or keep it/ in the museum it's impossible to see every room/ you have to promise to come back/ if they mixed up the artwork labels/ how long would people pretend/ how long would they see what's not there

Comedown

after Frank O'Hara

I'm a construction site abandoned to the rain   I need
    someone to know
I call my parents
I was out with some friends meaning

                         I'll never get to explain

you   on the other side of the footpath
already hours away   I could have tried harder but I
    couldn't

think of anything to say

the buzz is gone   the fridge is full of cold chips

I need to eat a whole punnet of grapes

I need to stand still feel the landscape move around me
like the painting the artist lets go

once on holidays my mum punched the sink
when my dad wouldn't get out of bed

I think I've forgotten something important

       in a conversation I'd like to get to the point
where either of us could excuse ourselves

start from there

Outing

they were ready to hear I wasn't ready to tell
I didn't want softness
lakes flashed by like mirrors either side of the road
my lasagne went cold in a takeaway box
I pretended to sleep
I dreamed I played them a song they pretended to like it
a motorbike overtook us the second man gripping the first's fleece
my mum asked had I known for long
my voice came from somewhere else
my dad went to the cinema then acted like nothing had changed
all summer I didn't know who knew
and how much
my uncle gave me a lift back to college
and played a whole opera on the radio

Lockdown Cycle

I haven't done something for the first
time in a long time so I grab my bike
from the shed wrench my saddle an inch
higher swing my leg around and pedal
off just out of reach of the ground my
feet circle I wobble like a bird on the
wire zipping between curb and tarmac
drain line I grip the handlebars with my
thumb fingers stretch to the brakes
screeching resistance slacken then
accelerate hedges ripple behind me I
pedal faster than my head spins faster
than the bending of speed around me my
roots rip back into something alive I
swerve onto the track by the river mud
spatters up up the levee now level with
sky and distant rooftops I plunge it's
nearly too much I keep going I pass a
thousand ideas I let them all go my bike
is a bike I cycle and just for a moment
between asphalt and blue I am me and
nothing else

Visit

We've cut through
a mountain,
tunnels, different
angles of
afternoon sunlight.
I've checked
my phone
fifteen times,
hugged every
guard on the way.
by the time I arrive
my heart will have
run so many laps
of my body
I'll need to take
off my shoes.
I miss you, if you want.
I bought a little plant
for you, it's spilling
crumbs of soil
in my bag.

ABOUT THE EDITOR

Leeanne Quinn

⌒

Leeanne Quinn is the author of two poetry collections. *Before You* (2012) was highly commended in the Forward Prize for Poetry 2013. Her second collection, *Some Lives*, was published in 2020 and noted as a Book of the Year by *The Irish Times* and *The Irish Independent*. With Joseph Woods, she co-edited *Romance Options*, an anthology of contemporary love poems from Ireland (Dedalus Press, 2022).

www.ingramcontent.com/pod-product-compliance
Lightning Source LLC
LaVergne TN
LVHW041202080426
835511LV00006B/714